How to Sell the Way Your Customer Buys

And Close the Sale Every Time

Des Hunt

www.tick.com.au

**How to Sell the Way Your Customer Buys
And Close the Sale Every Time**
Copyright © 1998 by Des Hunt. All rights reserved.

Published by:
Tick Concepts
PO Box 282 Kensington Park, South Australia 5068
Telephone: (08) 8463 1986
www.tick.com.au

National Library of Australia

ISBN: 978-0-9942084-0-8 (sc)
ISBN: 978-0-9942084-1-5 (ebk)

Also by the same author:

**"What Makes People Tick – How to Understand Yourself
and Others."**

"I Love You But How Do I Live With You"

*This book is dedicated to my sons-in-law Mark Ryan and
Glen Hansen. They are the sort of men I would have
chosen for sons.*

How to Sell the Way Your Customer Buys

And Close the Sale Every Time

Des Hunt

Des Hunt is an international speaker, trainer and seminar leader based in Australia. He is also the author of the best selling book *What Makes People Tick – How to Understand Yourself and Others.* He has been selling, and teaching others how to sell, for the best part of twenty-five years. Starting his working life on the workshop floor, he has held senior sales and marketing management positions as well as having run his own business employing over fifty people. He has studies in Marketing and Psychology, holds a Bachelor of Business degree and a Diploma in Training and Development.

For more products by Des Hunt visit:
www.tick.com.au

NOTICE TO TRAINERS AND HUMAN RESOURCE PROFESSIONALS

It is a breach of copyright and illegal to use any of the materials contained in this book including the bird symbols to depict personality styles.

Des Hunt's range of powerful training and human resource development materials and tools using the 'What Makes People Tick' principles and copyrighted bird symbols, are available for use under license to Human Resource professionals.

Part of these materials include the 'Personal Insight Profile Indicator Questionnaire' which is a far more comprehensive and accurate questionnaire than the one in this book, and is accompanied by the '16 Mini-Profiles Report' which are sold together as a pack.

Other materials available using the 'What Makes People Tick' principles and copyrighted bird graphics include notes on: Communicating, Team Building, Leading, Managing, Selling, Relationship Strategies and more.

For details on how to become a licensed user of the 'What Makes People Tick' materials contact:

Tick Concepts
PO Box 282 Kensington Park, South Australia 5068
Phone (08) 8463 1986
Email: info@tick.com.au
Website: www.tick.com.au

Contents

1

A quick word before we kick off

I hope that this doesn't look too much like a book. Because the best salespeople I have worked with, and who have worked for me, and whom I have trained over the years, generally don't like reading books.

In fact, it's been my experience that you have to threaten them with the gas chamber to even get them to do their paperwork — leave alone read a book.

So, my first and foremost job was to create something that was quick and easy to read and didn't look too much like a book. I hope I got it right.

I hope this doesn't look too much like a book.

I have been selling and training salespeople now for longer than I care to remember. Of all the sales training I attended when I first went into sales, and of all the training I have conducted over the years since, I believe that the principles outlined here are some of the most powerful that any salesperson can know and apply.

When I wrote the book *What Makes People Tick – How to Understand Yourself and Others,* it became a quiet best seller, and I'm happy to say it still continues to sell well and keeps me off the street.

Since writing *What Makes People Tick,* I have been approached by many people to write the book you now have in your hand, *How to Sell the Way Your Customer Buys* which is based on the *What Makes People Tick* principles, but is focused specifically on selling.

I guarantee that the principles work.

I can guarantee that the principles in this little book work.

I hope you read it. I hope you enjoy it.

More importantly, I hope you use it to boost your sales.

You are in one of the most important professions there is, because nothing happens until somebody sells something.

Every time you sell something, you keep another bunch of people in work.

You are in one of the most important professions in the world.

The politicians can talk forever about creating jobs, which is all they ever seem to do, but they will never be able to create jobs like you can.

So, do us all a favour — keep on selling.

Cheers,

Des Hunt
Adelaide 2008

And a word from Andrew Cole

I have been involved in sales for all of my professional life and I believe 'selling' to be the key to all transactions between people. You need to sell yourself in a job interview. You need to sell ideas in the workplace, as well as the traditional meaning of selling products and services.

This book is an easy read with some powerful messages to take away. It goes beyond the general theories of selling. It translates it right down to selling to individuals – which is really what selling is all about. It is based on the principles in Des Hunt's best-selling book, 'What Makes People Tick' which I would highly recommend you also read.

As a professional sales trainer with a background in sales dealing in multi-million dollar sales budgets, I utilise Des's simple models in all the training I deliver. Please read it, take just a few tips away to implement and see the changes to your results.

Andrew Cole
Adelaide 2008

2

People don't buy things, they buy how it will make them feel

Happy
Excited
Jealous
Anxious
Disturbed
Uncomfortable
Lonely
Guilty
Ashamed
Afraid
Frustrated
Uncertain
Hate
Revenge
Hostility
Greed
Patriotism
Love
Sad
Joyous
Suspicious
Bored
Embarrassed
Fear
Envy
Confused
Frightened

If you're thinking of selling using logic, forget it. People aren't logical creatures; they're feeling creatures.

We come out of the womb as feeling creatures and stay that way for the rest of our lives.

If human beings were logical we would all be wearing the same clothes, driving the same type of car, choosing partners that were the same, and none of us would drink or smoke.

Emotions and feelings are where it's at when it comes to knowing what makes people tick.

Logic only makes people think, it's emotions and feelings which make them act.

The First Law of Human Nature
The first law of human nature is: *People will move towards feelings that are pleasurable and move away from feelings that are painful.*

When was the last time you climbed the stairs instead of taking the lift?

When was the last time you chose to park your car a good step from the shop, rather than as close as you could get to the door?

When was the last time you sat in the front rows of a lecture theatre when the back rows were empty?

The reason we do things is all about pleasure and pain.

We are fairly clever when it comes to finding the right 'facts' to justify our feelings. We are good at making the facts fit our fictions.

To test the theory, simply involve somebody in a political, or religious, or any other discussion that they feel strongly about, and watch them find the 'facts' which supports their opinion-feelings.

The head will always find reasons for what the heart wants to do.

My friend the smoker points out people who have lived to a grand old age and who smoked all their lives.

Another way to test the theory is to listen to someone who has paid too much for something justify why they paid so much. We can justify murder if it fits in with our feelings.

People are Happiness-Seeking Creatures

We spend our lives trying to have our wants satisfied.

Almost everything we do and say is to fulfil a want.

It could be said that we are a bunch of wants in constant search of having them satisfied. And when they are satisfied, it gives our lives a sense of meaning and purpose.

Happiness is having our wants satisfied.

Happiness is having our wants satisfied.

- ◆ **Good health**
- ◆ **Food**
- ◆ **Shelter**
- ◆ **Safety**
- ◆ **Comfort**
- ◆ **Sex**
- ◆ **Security**
- ◆ **Love**
- ◆ **Friendship**
- ◆ **Achievement**
- ◆ **Acceptance**
- ◆ **Predictability**
- ◆ **Control**
- ◆ **Recognition**
- ◆ **Self-fulfilment**

PLEASURE	PAIN
Health	Sickness
Easy to do	Hard to do
Economical	Expensive
Convenient	Inconvenient
Familiar	Unknown
Security	Insecurity
In control	No control
Saves time	Wastes time
Reliable	Unreliable
Safe	Dangerous
Loved	Unloved
Accepted	Rejected
Relaxed	Disturbed
Independence	Dependence
Peace of mind	Confusion
Comfortable	Uncomfortable

People are Not Logical

We do things because they feel right, not because they are logical.

We make the facts fit anything we want them to fit.

Logic is a *need*, feelings are a *want*. As a friend of mine said to me not long ago, "I really need to give up smoking. There are a dozen logical reasons why I should give it up, it will eventually kill me is a pretty good logical reason alone, but there is just one thing stopping me, I don't *want* to." A *want* will win every time over a *need*.

We Make the Facts Fit Our Feelings

We can make the facts fit anything we want them to fit.

FOOD FOR THOUGHT

People only ever buy two things:

The answer to a problem

and

Good feelings

Nobody has ever made a purely logical decision to buy anything.

People don't buy low-fat foods; they buy attractiveness and acceptance.

People don't buy health care products; they buy well-being and a longer life.

People don't buy photographs; they buy pleasurable memories.

People don't buy locks; they buy safety and security.

People don't buy microwave ovens; they buy speed and convenience.

People don't buy designer clothes; they buy recognition and importance.

People don't buy insurance; they buy peace of mind.

People don't buy holidays; they buy relaxation and pleasure.

People don't buy cars; they buy speed, convenience and ego.

People don't buy cosmetics; they buy youth and beauty.

People don't buy gifts; they buy love, friendship and approval.

People don't buy steak; they buy taste and pleasure.

People don't buy electric drills; they buy fast holes.

People don't buy things; they buy good feelings.

Feelings are the Hidden Persuaders.

Let's have a closer look at them in the next chapter.

The Hidden Persuaders

3

The top 20 hit songs on WIIFM

It's been said that we think about ourselves ninety-eight per cent of the time, and I wouldn't argue with that.

Whether we like it, or not, we human beings are fairly self-centred creatures. We are all glued in to Radio Station WIIFM — "What's In It For Me?"

We all listen to Radio Station WIIFM.

The Top 20 hit songs on Radio Station WIIFM, the ones we like to hear, are the Hidden Persuaders.

They are the major feelings and wants that move us. They're the ones we really tune into. Here is the hit list:

1. I want to live forever
2. I want to be healthy
3. The sex drive
4. I want life to be easy
5. I want to be like you
6. I want to get something for nothing
7. I don't want to worry about losing something
8. I worry about what I don't know
9. I want to have security
10. I want to be loved and belong
11. I want to feel important

If you want to persuade me, make sure you play the songs I want to hear

12. I want to feel attractive
13. I want to be in control
14. I want to possess things
15. I want recreation and relaxation
16. If it's scarce, I want it more
17. I don't want to feel obligated
18. I take notice of what the experts say
19. I fear anything threatening
20. I want to believe in a higher power

Let's have a quick and closer look at them:

1. I want to live forever
The most basic of the human wants; self-survival.

When was the last time you saw a doctor go broke?

If you want me to do what you're asking me to do, and it helps me to live longer, then you've got me.

When was the last time you saw a doctor, or a pharmacy, go broke?

2. I want to be healthy
The second most basic of the human wants; to be healthy.

Low fat, sugar free, no calories, no nuttin'.

The health food industry is a multi-billion industry. You don't have to be Stephen Hawking to know that this one rates in the top 3 of the Hit Parade.

3. The sex drive

Birds do it, bees do it...

The third most basic of the human wants; the sex drive. Sex sells.

As if you didn't already know that!

4. I want life to be easy

Quicker, faster, easier...

People will do almost anything to avoid discomfort exertion and inconvenience.

Finding a closer parking space, mobile phones, microwave ovens, and hating to wait in queues are just some examples.

We want life to be easy. That's why McDonalds is so popular and profitable.

5. I want to be like you

We want to imitate. From fashions, to cars, to social fads, we copy each other. Imitation is a powerful mover.

That's why personalities and film stars are paid heaps to endorse products.

You're nobody if you don't wear Nike.

6. I want to get something for nothing

Discounts, freebies, bonus packs, getting a bargain, or better still, something free, is irresistible.

Perhaps the best example of all is gambling. In 1996-97, Australians wagered just under $80 billion on all forms of gambling.

We all want to get something for nothing.

And not only that ... you also get twelve free steak knives!

7. I don't want to worry about losing something

Most people don't like to take risks. We are motivated more by the fear of losing something than by the pleasure of gaining something. This is why the insurance industry is so big.

We fear losing our life, our time, our health, our security, our jobs, our reputation — you name losing it and we fear it.

If you want to see a demonstration of this in action, watch people shopping before a long-weekend. You'd think the shops were going to be closed forever!

"But what if...?

8. I worry about what I don't know

Most people will opt for the known and the familiar, rather than take a risk with the unknown.

'Worry,' that thing that all us human beings tend to do, is simply the fear of the unknown. That's why tried and proven things are always easier to sell.

"Better the dog you know than the one you don't know."

9. I want to have security

This the first cousin to 'the fear of losing something.'

We want life to be predictable. We like the comfort of the familiar. No unpleasant surprises.

We want a 'sure bet'. We want guarantees.

"Okay, what's the catch?"

10. I want to be loved and belong

We humans are tribal creatures. We fear being an outsider.

I wanna be part of the gang.

We want to belong, to be accepted as part of the family, the group, the club, the organisation, and most of all we want to be loved.

We see good examples of this mover in the peer pressure of the street gang, in the conformity to the rules of organisations, right through to national cultures (unwritten rules), to patriotism.

11. I want to feel important

We all want to feel valued and important.

We all want to feel valued and worthy — that we are making a contribution.

That car's a real head-turner.

Some of us have a bigger need than others. Watch the Logies and the Acadamy Awards presentations.

Some examples (and there are plenty more) of this mover are; designer label clothes (once we used to wear the labels inside of our clothes!), status symbols, 'image products,' public recognition, name-dropping, fame, and any 'look at me' behaviour.

But it's not only limited the 'showy.' It also takes in workaholism and people acting like a martyr above and beyond the call of duty.

12. I want to feel attractive

We all like to feel that we are attractive to others.

G'day you sexy thing.

Being attracted to each other is what makes the world go around. Without it there would be no love, no friendships, no sex — and no future generations!

Examples of this mover at work are; Gyms and health clubs, diet foods and drinks, potions and creams to make us look younger, cosmetics, hair transplants, right through to plastic surgery.

13. I want to be in control

We all like to be in control — of ourselves and life.

Some like to be in control of everything.

Not only do some of these people want to be in control of themselves, but they also want to be in control of everybody else.

Some examples of this mover are; competitiveness, winning at all costs, intimidation and the need to dominate others.

The 'want to control' can also be seen when people buy more powerful, or larger, things than they really need — such as cars, boats, power tools, motor cycles and the like. A good example are the four-wheel drive 'Toorak Tanks' that have never been off the bitumen.

You can now buy a motorbike with a 350 Chevy V8 engine in it. No household should be without one!

14. I want to possess things

This is the want to have something for no other reason than to have it.

This is the big one that makes modern marketing what it is.

If you want to see a good example of this mover, check out the things around your home that you bought once but don't really need and now wonder why you ever bought them in the first place.

Better still, try moving house!

Marketing is the art of making people long for something their grandparents never heard of and probably lived very happily without.

15. I want recreation and relaxation

This is the first cousin to 'I want life to be easy.'

This is the want that literally means to 're-create.'

Often marketed under the name of 'lifestyle,' it takes in the want for enjoyment, change, stimulus, and doing something different, having fun and enjoyment.

Examples of this want can be seen in; hobbies, holidays, travelling, eating out, sport, leisure activities, theatre, movies, parties and celebrations.

The top 5 Australian leisure activities are:
1. Watching TV.
2. Listening to the radio.
3. Reading.
4. Visiting friends.
5. Listening to music.

16. If it's scarce, I want it more

Have you noticed how things become more attractive and valuable if they are rare, scarce, or we think we can't have them?

If we think we might miss out on something, we want it even more.

This is a strictly limited offer. No more will be produced after these are sold.

Don't do me any favours.

17. I don't want to feel obligated

The guilt of obligation is a powerful mover.

If you do, then I must do. I must return the favour.

I must 'do the right thing' — otherwise I owe you something. I am in debt to you and feel obligated until the favour is returned.

"I think there is a world market for perhaps about five computers." IBM Chairman, Tom Watson, 1944.

18. I take notice of what the experts say

We put a lot of faith in what 'experts' tell us.

Throughout history we have been persuaded by the opinions of experts.

We tend to follow the lead of experts and authorities, irrespective of whether they are right or wrong. And a good many are proved to be wrong, but we still listen and take notice of the next one who tells us what it is that we should, or should not, be doing.

Every year, 1 in 5 Australians suffer a nervous breakdown.

19. I fear anything threatening

This is part of the family of the 'fear of losing something,' the 'fear of the unknown,' and the 'fear of pain.'

The security industry makes billions with this mover.

80 million people have died as a direct result of war in this century alone mainly caused through the cry of: "For God and country!"

20. I want to believe in a higher power

Faith, they say, can move mountains.

A powerful human want is the need to believe in a higher power, and a life hereafter.

Religion is a booming and very profitable industry.

Add faith to patriotism and you have one of the most potent human movers in the history of mankind.

FOOD FOR THOUGHT

Don't tell me
what it will do

Tell me how
it will make
me feel

Sell the payoffs
not the product

To sum up this chapter

People buy feelings, not products.

When you can align what you're selling with the major movers — the WIIFM's — of your buyer, you have grasped the key to selling anything.

Later on, we'll have a look at just who likes what, WIIFM's. But for now, let's pull this chapter together.

Here are some of the hit song WIIFM's applied to a product and expressed in street language.

- It adds years to your life.
- Makes you feel vital and alive.
- Saves you time and money.
- Makes you money.
- Safe to use anywhere.
- Simple, quick and easy to use.
- All the famous people are using it.
- A free bonus pack comes with it.
- Full money back guarantee.
- No more worries or stress.
- A secure gilt-edged investment.
- Your friends will love you for it.
- For the most important people in your life.
- Show you are a discerning buyer.
- Don't settle for second best.
- You deserve it.
- You'll turn heads with this one.
- Puts you in control.
- This is a rare and limited offer.
- Owning it is a joy to have.
- Enjoy it every day.
- No obligation free trial period.
- Approved by leading experts.
- Tough and durable.
- Maintenance free.
- Proven performance
- Total back-up service.
- Proven brand name.
- Value for money.

The four big WIIFM's

4

We've talked about the Top 20 WIIFM's. Now it's time to look at the 'Big Four WIIFM's'.

These are the deep motivating drivers. These are the things which dictate our words and actions. These are the things which make us who we are.

The things that make us who we are.

But before we look at these it will pay us to to get a better bead on human nature. After all, selling is the 'people business' and if we want to do a lot better than average in selling, it will pay us to understand people a whole lot better.

So, some guiding principles. Some of them I have mentioned before, but they are worth repeating here:

♦ We think about ourselves ninety-eight per cent of the time.
♦ People do things for their reasons, not yours.
♦ People do things because they feel right, not because they are right.
♦ No matter how stupid it looks to you, it always makes sense to the person doing it.

It always makes sense to the person doing it.

♦ Almost everything we do and say is to fulfil a want that is important to us.
♦ We will always move towards pleasurable feelings and away from painful feelings.
♦ When you can align what you're selling with the wants of the buyer you can sell anything.

Taking for granted, and ignoring the most basic wants of food, shelter and safety — the 'animal needs' which we share with other creatures, the big four wants are:

1. The security of predictability
2. Love, friendship and belonging
3. Recognition, praise and applause
4. Control, authority and power

These are the things which deeply move us.

1. The security of predictability

Whilst we all like a bit of structure and predictability in our lives, there are those who are almost junkies on it.

What does the instruction manual say?

These are the people that do everything by the book, the rules, the law. They actually read instruction manuals!

They are governed internally by systems and habits. They do things in the same way, each time, every time.

They write lists for everything. Nothing is left to chance.

They are uncomfortable with change, leave alone anything that appears risky — which is a lot of things to these people.

The pessimists of life, they are always looking for the catch. They want the sure bet and the guarantees.

They want the nitty gritty details of everything.

I call these people *Owls* and we'll get to know them and how to pick them later.

2. Love, friendship and belonging

We all want to be loved and we all want friends, but there are some people who would have a nervous breakdown if they didn't have them.

I know you hate me, but can't we be friends?

These are the shy and quiet people of life. Often called 'the salt of the earth,' they would do anything for you.

Totally supportive, they're more than happy to go along with the cowd.

Always with a willing ear for other peoples' problems, they are caring and lovable. I call these people *Doves*. We'll meet them properly later.

3. Recognition, praise and applause
We all like a bit of recognition and praise, but there are some of us who can't live without it.

These are the people who might be seen as 'showy' and 'flashy.'

One thing is for sure, you will know they're around. They never stop talking.

Hey baby, if you've got it – flaunt it.

Big on name-dropping, if you don't ask them, they'll tell you how good they are.

They're big on displaying status symbols, and they've got them whether they can afford them or not.

I call these people the **Peacocks** and I'll show you how to pick them and sell to them later.

4. Control, authority and power
You can't blame anyone for wanting a bit of control, but there are some people that want to take over the world!

These are the no-nonsense, businesslike people. Fast and to the point, they always seem to have somebody more important to talk to than you.

I'm the boss here and don't you forget it!

Blunt and to the point, they always want to know what the bottom line is as soon as you open your mouth.

Because they love authority, you will find plenty of them in senior management positions.

Extremely competitive, life is a grim game of win at all costs.

I call these people the **Eagles** and we'll have the pleasure of their company later.

So, let's now get to know them so that we can pick them and sell to them the way that they want to buy.

5 Getting to know the styles

The Peacock

The Dove

The Eagle

The Owl

"Yeah, G'Day, Howyagoin' mate? I'm the Peacock and you know plenty of people just like me. I can talk the leg off a chair and know all the latest gags. I'm the life of the party, people just love me. I'm witty, good fun to be with and popular with just about everyone, although I must admit those boring Owls see me as a bit of a loud-mouth — but what would they know. Sure, I like to talk and wear the latest fashions. If you've got it, flaunt it, is what I always say. I'll catch you later, but before I go, have you heard the one about ..."

The Peacock

"Hello there, how are you? And how is your family, well, I hope. I'm the Dove. I'm gentle and modest, and when I'm with strangers I can be quite shy. But when I'm with my friends, I can talk the leg off a pot. People tell me I'm caring and very supportive, but I don't know about that. All I do know is that friends and family are very important, and if you can't help somebody out, what's the point of it all. I love just about everyone, but I must admit I find those Eagles a little too abrupt and bossy for my liking. By the way, how is that sick aunty of yours?"

The Dove

"Yes, hello. I'm the Eagle, or so they tell me. I'm not much into all this psychology crap. I just get on with the job. Sure, I like to be the boss. You can't make things happen, you can't get results if you're not in a position of some authority. By the way, what's the time? I've got an important appointment in twelve minutes, so we'll have to keep this short. Competitive? Sure, I'm competitive. Winners are grinners. This business about 'it's how you play the game, rather than wanting to win' is a load of crap in my book. See you later. I'm busy — got to rush."

The Eagle

The Owl

"Good morning, how are you today? So, they say I am an Owl do they? Well I don't know about that. What I can say is that I'm very careful and cautious, conservative you might say. I certainly like to know what I'm getting myself in to. You won't see me rushing in where wise men fear to tread — not like those impulsive rush-in-and-think-after Peacock types. I like to know the details. I think long and hard about any decisions I make. I also like things to be on paper. I find that there are some people who have convenient memories. If it's on paper, you can't go wrong. Well, that's my opinion anyway."

I'm a talker – I'm a Peacock

I'm a Feeler – I'm a Dove

I'm a Doer – I'm an Eagle

I'm a Thinker – I'm an Owl

Communication styles

THE PEACOCK
Talks fast
Strong voice
Expressive face
Dramatic gestures
Witty
Poor listener
Interrupts speaker
They talk about themselves

THE DOVE
Softly spoken
Self-conscious
Bashful
Modest
Expressive face
Easy to talk to
Good listener
They ask you how you are

THE EAGLE
Talks fast
To the point
No nonsense
No small talk
Can seem blunt
Poor listener
Interrupts speaker
They tell you what to do

THE OWL
Softly spoken
Quiet and serious
Non-expressive face
Can seem detached
Slow to respond
Good listener
Can be a closed book
They talk about the details

Driving wants
What I really love

THE PEACOCK
I want achievement
I want recognition
I want praise
I want applause
I want to be noticed
I want status
I want to be famous!

THE DOVE
I want security
I want to belong
I want to be loved
I want a quiet life
I want peace
I want harmony
I want to be your friend

THE EAGLE
I want achievement
I want authority
I want challenge
I want to get results
I want to be obeyed
I want it quick
I want to be the boss!

THE OWL
I want security
I want structure
I want systems
I want rules
I want law and order
I want life to be predictable
I want to be right

Absolute turn-offs
What I really hate

THE PEACOCK
I hate not being noticed
I hate being criticized
I hate paperwork
I hate discipline
I hate bureaucracies
I hate having no one to talk to
I hate being bored

THE DOVE
I hate rejection
I hate over-bearing people
I hate aggressiveness
I hate conflict
I hate being taken for granted
I hate making decisions
I hate taking risks

THE EAGLE
I hate not getting my own way
I hate having to obey others
I hate being dependent
I hate inaction
I hate wimps
I hate excuses
I hate losing

THE OWL
I hate uncertainty
I hate salespeople
I hate impulsiveness
I hate taking risks
I hate having no system
I hate making quick decisions
I hate change

The Peacock at a glance

Other Names	The Persuader, The Promotor, The Actor, The Motivator.
Wants	Popularity and fame.
Theme Song	"Hey world – look at me!"
Dress	Stylish, colourful, designer labels, flamboyant.
Can Be Seen As	Loud, showy, superficial, talks too much.
Communicates	Outspoken, unselfconscious, fast and expressive.
Loves	Popularity — being in the limelight.
Hates	Not being noticed. Not getting recognition.
Good As	Salespeople, Entertainers, Speakers, Promoters.
Not Good At	Emotional control, analysing, listening, punctuality.
Strengths	Persuasive, energetic, creative, optimistic.
Shortcomings	Undisciplined, exaggerates, manipulative, self-centred.
Fears	Not being noticed, permanence, sameness, being bored.
Motivated By	Recognition, applause, status symbols, fame.
Often feels	Angry and frustrated.
Under Pressure	Becomes noisy and dramatic, then wants to be friends.

The Peacock at a glance

I Can't	"I can't live without being different."
Other Peacocks	Kylie Minogue, Bob Hawke, Paul Hogan, Bill Clinton, Madonna, Shane Warne, Superman, Dolly Parton, Cher.
Peacock Countries	America and Italy – and Sydney.
As Seen By The Owl	A chronically loud-mouthed showoff, emotionally immature, a dummy-spitter, showy, impulsive, scatter-brained, talks too much, no substance, no good with paperwork, open their mouths to change feet, half as good as they think they are.
Buys	Anything that makes them look good, irrespective of whether or not they can afford it. Will often go into debt just for the sake of 'image.'

The Dove at a glance

Other Names	The Supporter, The Peacemaker, The Amiable.
Wants	To belong, love and friendship. Harmony.
Theme Song	"We all need each other – and let's save the whales."
Dress	Pastel to bright colours, but not outlandish.
Can Be Seen As	Unmotivated, soft, easily lead, over-sensitive.
Communicates	Softly spoken, self-conscious, quiet, bashful.
Loves	Acceptance and approval. A quiet life.
Hates	Rejection, aggressive people and conflict situations.
Good As	Team workers, customer service, social workers.
Not Good At	Being independent, leading, making decisions.
Strengths	Compassionate, friendly, loyal, patient.
Shortcomings	Unsure, depedent, over compliant, easily led.
Fears	Having to go it alone.
Motivated By	Acceptance, approval, belonging. Peace and harmony.
Often Feels	Inadequate.
Under Pressure	Withdraws, then becomes quietly stubborn.

The Dove at a glance

I Can't	"I can't live without being accepted and loved."
Other Doves	Queen Mother, Lady Diana, Marj Simpson, Jerry Seinfeld.
Dove Countries	Malaysia and New Guinea – and Brisbane.
As Seen By The Eagle	Chronically wimpy and nice, totally unmotivated, easily led, worries too much about what other people think.
Buys	Anything that makes them and theirs happy, generally a careful shopper – thinks twice.

The Eagle at a glance

Other Names	The Controller, The Enforcer, The Dominator.
Wants	Authority and control – to be productive.
Theme Song	"Winning isn't everything – it's the only thing."
Dress	Darker colours, smart but conservative.
Can Be Seen As	Bossy, aggressive, arrogant, pushy, impatient.
Communicates	Strong voice, quick, abrupt, to the point.
Loves	Winning – achievement – getting results.
Hates	Losing.
Good As	Project managers, military leaders, leader of Hell's Angels.
Not Good At	Tolerance, teamwork, diplomacy, being patient.
Strengths	Productive, independent, confident, decisive.
Shortcomings	Autocratic, unbending, impatient, critical, undiplomatic.
Fears	Not being in control.
Motivated By	Challenge, action, competition, getting results.
Often Feels	Worried.
Under Pressure	Bossy and sarcastic, then avoids the situation or person.

The Eagle at a glance

I Can't	"I can't live without goals and achievement."
Other Eagles	Margaret Thatcher, Rupert Murdoch, Kerry Packer, Greg Norman, The Queen, Batman.
Eagle Countries	Singapore and Russia – and Melbourne.
As Seen By The Dove	A chronic bossy dictator, suffers from toxic bossiness, makes Attila the Hun look like a boy scout, Margaret Thatcher on steroids.
Buys	Fast and decisively.

The Owl at a glance

Other Names	The Analyser, The Thinker, The Pessimist, The Perfectionist.
Wants	Order and predictability — certainty.
Theme Song	"Fools rush in where wise men fear to tread."
Dress	Browns and autumn colours, very conservative.
Can Be Seen As	Unsociable, fussy, picky, critical and a pain for details.
Communicates	Softly spoken, unemotional, detached, preoccupied.
Loves	Certainty.
Hates	Surprises – good or bad.
Good As	Accountants, Scientists, Engineers, Quality Control.
Not Good At	Socialising, interacting, quick decisions, taking risks.
Strengths	Careful, thorough, exact, systematic, consistent.
Shortcomings	Over-cautious, negative, indecisive, self-righteous, inflexible.
Fears	Uncertainty - and imperfection – and change.
Motivated By	Procedures, information, rules, predictability.
Often Feels	Inadequate.
Under Pressure	Becomes quietly critical and then withdraws within.

The Owl at a glance

I Can't	"I can't live with imperfection."
Other Owls	Albert Einstein, Prince Charles, Clark Kent, John Howard (ex Australian Prime Minister) and most bank managers!
Owl Countries	England and Switzerland – and Adelaide.
As Seen By The Peacock	A terminally serious up-tight person, has had a personality by-pass, completely colourless, you ask them the time and they will tell you how a clock works.
Buys	Very practical shopper, only buys the tried and proven, subscribes to 'Choice' magazine.

6 How to pick the styles

Within 30 seconds of meeting them

We are communicating who we are all the time.

W̲e are communicating all the time. In fact, we cannot *not* communicate.

We tell each other who we are in three very distinct ways, and they are:

1. By how we look
2. By what we say
3. By how we say it

In these three ways we communicate to the world whether we are:

We communicate to the world the way we want to be communicated to.

- ♦ Confident and assertive, or
- ♦ Shy and retiring
- ♦ Friendly and warm, or
- ♦ Cool and distant

We communicate with the world the way we want to be communicated to.

The Peacock
Confident and assertive – friendly and warm.
Speed: Fast.
Face: Open, expressive and cheerful.
Acts: Relaxed and friendly.
What and How: Lots of colourful language and dramatic expression. They talk about themselves.

The Dove
Shy and retiring – friendly and warm.
Speed: Slow.
Face: Bashful, expressions reflect what you are saying.
Acts: Like a friendly listener.
What and How: Easygoing, talks quietly and calmly. They ask about your wellbeing. Lots of small talk.

The Eagle
Confident and assertive – cool and distant.
Speed: Fast.
Face: Set and determined, gives little away.
Acts: In a quick and businesslike manner.
What and How: Sticks to the task at hand. Wants 'the bottom line.' Little, or no, small talk.

The Owl
Shy and retiring – cool and distant.
Speed: Slow.
Face: Expressionless, sometimes grim.
Acts: Quiet and withdrawn, preoccupied.
What and How: Precise, sticks to the facts. Asks questions. Uncomfortable with small talk.

How to pick the styles in a nutshell

Friendly
Warm
Easygoing

Confident
Assertive
Talker
Fast

Shy
Retiring
Listener
Slow

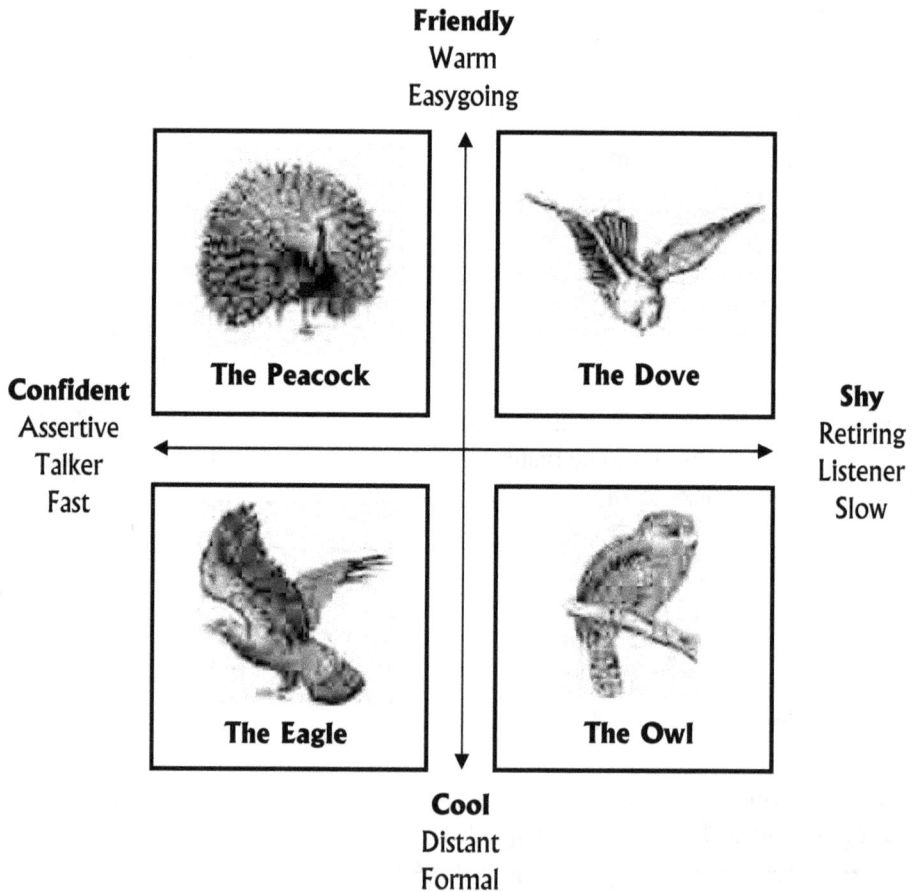

The Peacock

The Dove

The Eagle

The Owl

Cool
Distant
Formal

How to pick the styles by their work spaces

Whether we know it, or not, we all create personal environments that are comfortable for us, and in turn, reflect our style.

It is no coincidence that a Peacock's personal space generally looks as if a bomb has gone off – there is stuff everywhere.

Our personal spaces reflect our style.

It is also no coincidence that an Owl's personal space is generally neat and tidy. And if there is lots of stuff around, it is generally in neat piles and he or she knows just where everything is.

The male Owls are the sort of people who have those boards on the wall of their garage with the pictures of the tools drawn on them.

The male Peacock may also have the board with the pictures in his garage. The big difference between the two is that in the Owl's garage all the tools will be on the pictures. In the Peacock's garage the pictures will be empty, the tools all over the place, and half of them missing anyway!

As most of our selling is done in a business environment, I'll stick to work scenarios for showing you how to pick a style from the way their work and office environment look.

After a little practise, when you get good at it, you can pick the style, whether they are there, or not, simply by having a good look around.

Keep your eyes open and look for the clues.

This is especially handy when you are ushered into their office and they're not there. "Mr. Jones will be with you in a minute." Start looking for clues.

The Peacock's space

The Peacock will have his, or her, achievements on display. A photo of a good-looking partner will be on the desk - facing you. But if they aren't good-looking, then the photo will be in the drawer! Certificates of accomplishments will hang on the wall, along with photos of themselves with semi-famous people. The books in the shelves will be non-technical. The office will be messy, unless they've just had a hurried tidy-up in order to look good and create the right image.

The Dove's space

The Dove's office is homely. There is generally a separate little area with a coffee table and chairs which is used for talking to visitors. (Talking from behind a desk is impersonal). A photo of the family, complete with family dog will be on display. Posters like 'When we work as a team we can achieve miracles' will be on the wall. Somewhere in the office will invariably be a potted plant.

The Eagle's space

Unless they've had an interior decorator to do their office, it generally looks just like them − strictly a place of business. There are no frills. There are no softening features. They do their business from behind a desk. The desk is neat and well organised, sometimes even appearing bare. There will be a clock in view. On the wall will be a yearly planner with those stick-on arrows and dots. The whole office says 'This person is organised!'

The Owl's space

The Owl's office will either look like an operating theatre, or it will have piles of paper all over the place, but it will still appear 'organised.' In the bookshelves are technical manuals. On the wall is a graph with lines showing the rises and falls of something. There will be little, or no, 'personal effects' evident.

A guide to picking the styles

Picking people's styles has become second nature and instinctive with me now – I don't even think about it.

For those with 'L plates' on, the best way to do it on meeting someone is to ask yourself, "What are they *not?*" In other words, do it by the process of elimination.

Do it by the process of elimination.

After looking for what they are not, then start looking for what they *are* to confirm you have picked the right style. For example:

Look for what they are not first.

Does he look me straight in the eye when I speak to him? No. Well I must be dealing with a Dove, or an Owl.

Is he fast and confident in his approach to me? No. OK, I'm still dealing with a Dove, or an Owl.

Is he amiable, warm and friendly? Relaxed? No. Well he's not a Dove. I think I'm dealing with an Owl.

Confirm by looking for what they are.

Is he poker-faced with little body language, dressed conservatively? Yes. Does he seem distant, impersonal? Yes. I'm definitely dealing with an Owl.

I would immediately go into 'Owl mode' and start to sell the way the Owl buys – but I'm getting ahead of myself.

Eight out of ten ain't bad

Keep in mind that this a guide to the galaxy of human nature.

You will never be able to pick them all. And that's good. It would be awful if all of us fitted neatly into little boxes. But you should be able to pick eight out of every ten people you meet – and eight out of ten ain't bad.

Combinations of the styles

We could get carried away and start talking about the different combinations – Peacock-Eagles, Owl-Doves etc. – and finish up with sixteen style combinations, but that's not the purpose of this book.

We are only talking about the four basic styles.

If you want to go deeper.

If you would like to go into it to that sort of depth, then my other book, *What Makes People Tick*, is the book to go to.

What Makes People Tick not only contains a full description of each of the sixteen combinations, but also has an in-depth self-scoring questionnaire that you can use to pinpoint your own style and see how it can be perceived by others.

Good ideas only work if you do.

As I said, that's only if you want to go deeper. Simply becoming familiar with the four basic styles, and then using what you know, will increase your selling effectiveness ten-fold. But, like all good ideas, they don't work unless you do.

A guide to your own style

Without going into the depth that I go into in my book *What Makes People Tick*, I have included in the next chapter a quick questionnaire that you can use that should give you a fair idea of your style.

See yourself as others see you.

I have also included a variation of the same questionnaire that you can give to your friends to fill out so that you can see both how others see you, and how it compares with your own view of yourself.

A guide to your own style

7

For most of us, we are a combination of the four basic styles.

But when we are in our comfort zones (when we are being our 'natural selves') we usually operate out of only two styles. These are our 'two prefered styles.'

And of these two prefered styles we usually dominate in one — as a Peacock, a Dove, an Eagle, or an Owl.

Operating out of our prefered dominant style is our way of making some sense out of the world.

Seeing the world from our most dominant style helps us makes sense of it.

Of course the world forces us to be different people at different times. We act the part we are supposed to play. But being human, we will always want to return to our comfort zones, to being our natural selves. You can only act a part for so long.

We will always return to our comfort zone.

And even while acting the part, we are still driven by the values and beliefs which drive our natural style.

How I see myself

Tick the words on the lists below which you think best describe you. Do not tick more than 40 or less than 20. And be honest with yourself.

☐ outgoing	☐ caring
☐ outspoken	☐ passive
☐ enthusiastic	☐ calm
☐ motivating	☐ modest
☐ optimistic	☐ gentle
☐ flamboyant	☐ sincere
☐ charming	☐ helpful
☐ imaginative	☐ easygoing
☐ persuasive	☐ even tempered
☐ unselfconscious	☐ pleasant
☐ carefree	☐ friendly
☐ impulsive	☐ good listener
☐ talkative	☐ shy
☐ spontaneous	☐ sympathetic
☐ friendly	☐ supportive
☐ exaggerates	☐ trusting
☐ animated	☐ dependable
☐ humorous	☐ kind
☐ dramatic	☐ peaceful
☐ lively	☐ warm hearted
☐ excitable	☐ easygoing
☐ energetic	☐ unassuming
☐ visual	☐ sensitive
☐ entertaining	☐ co-operative

P

D

How I see myself

- ☐ forceful
- ☐ cool
- ☐ independent
- ☐ businesslike
- ☐ competitive
- ☐ critical
- ☐ assertive
- ☐ bold
- ☐ decisive
- ☐ self-reliant
- ☐ efficient
- ☐ bossy
- ☐ impatient
- ☐ blunt
- ☐ productive
- ☐ workaholic
- ☐ unbending
- ☐ decisive
- ☐ tough
- ☐ determined
- ☐ ambitious
- ☐ domineering
- ☐ strong-willed
- ☐ aggressive

E ☐

- ☐ conservative
- ☐ analytical
- ☐ practical
- ☐ reliable
- ☐ quiet
- ☐ stable
- ☐ detached
- ☐ systematic
- ☐ predictable
- ☐ perfectionist
- ☐ reserved
- ☐ loner
- ☐ unemotional
- ☐ pessimistic
- ☐ careful
- ☐ fussy
- ☐ stiff
- ☐ precise
- ☐ patient
- ☐ diplomatic
- ☐ efficient
- ☐ restrained
- ☐ unsociable
- ☐ indecisive

O ☐

Now add up the totals in each column to reveal your prefered and dominant styles. The highest score is your most dominant style.

P column is Peacock style

D column is Dove style

E column is Eagle style

O column is Owl style

How others see me

Tick the words on the lists below which you think best describe me. Do not tick more than 40 or less than 20. And be honest — I can take it!

☐ outgoing	☐ caring
☐ outspoken	☐ passive
☐ enthusiastic	☐ calm
☐ motivating	☐ modest
☐ optimistic	☐ gentle
☐ flamboyant	☐ sincere
☐ charming	☐ helpful
☐ imaginative	☐ easygoing
☐ persuasive	☐ even tempered
☐ unselfconscious	☐ pleasant
☐ carefree	☐ friendly
☐ impulsive	☐ good listener
☐ talkative	☐ shy
☐ spontaneous	☐ sympathetic
☐ friendly	☐ supportive
☐ exaggerates	☐ trusting
☐ animated	☐ dependable
☐ humorous	☐ kind
☐ dramatic	☐ peaceful
☐ lively	☐ warm hearted
☐ excitable	☐ easygoing
☐ energetic	☐ unassuming
☐ visual	☐ sensitive
☐ entertaining	☐ co-operative

P ▢

D ▢

How others see me

- ☐ forceful
- ☐ cool
- ☐ independent
- ☐ businesslike
- ☐ competitive
- ☐ critical
- ☐ assertive
- ☐ bold
- ☐ decisive
- ☐ self-reliant
- ☐ efficient
- ☐ bossy
- ☐ impatient
- ☐ blunt
- ☐ productive
- ☐ workaholic
- ☐ unbending
- ☐ decisive
- ☐ tough
- ☐ determined
- ☐ ambitious
- ☐ domineering
- ☐ strong-willed
- ☐ aggressive

E

- ☐ conservative
- ☐ analytical
- ☐ practical
- ☐ reliable
- ☐ quiet
- ☐ stable
- ☐ detached
- ☐ systematic
- ☐ predictable
- ☐ perfectionist
- ☐ reserved
- ☐ loner
- ☐ unemotional
- ☐ pessimistic
- ☐ careful
- ☐ fussy
- ☐ stiff
- ☐ precise
- ☐ patient
- ☐ diplomatic
- ☐ efficient
- ☐ restrained
- ☐ unsociable
- ☐ indecisive

O

Thank you for helping me see myself as others see me. I'll let you know later whether or not I'm happy about it!

FOOD FOR THOUGHT

Tomorrow
will be no
different to
yesterday if
you don't
change what
you're doing
today

The 7 principles and laws of selling the way your customer buys

8

There has been an awful lot written and spoken about how to, and how not to, sell.

I don't intend to reinvent the wheel here, but I do believe there are some principles and laws well worth keeping in mind.

So, before we get to actually selling to the different styles, let's have a look at what I think are the seven principles of selling, along with their accompanying seven unbreakable laws.

I'm sure you've gathered by now that I'm not talking to those people who call themselves 'salespeople' but don't really sell anything.

In other words, I'm not talking to those 'salespeople' who work in situations where people buy things irrespective of who 'sells' it to them – they probably wouldn't be reading this book anyway.

I'm talking to you, the professional salesperson, who wants to enhance your knowledge and skills, and hone your craft like any other true professional.

So here are the seven principles and laws of selling the way your customer buys as I see it.

I don't intend to reinvent the wheel.

I'm not talking to those people who call themselves salespeople but don't really sell anything.

Guiding Principle	Accompanying Law
Principle 1: People do things for their reasons, not yours and they always will.	**Law 1:** Always sell based on the customer's reasons, not your own.
Principle 2: Selling is more about opening than it is about closing.	**Law 2:** Your first job is to get people to like you.
Principle 3: People generally buy from people they trust and feel comfortable with.	**Law 3:** Adapt quickly to your customer's style.
Principle 4: People don't buy things, they buy how it will make them feel.	**Law 4:** Find out what your customer is buying, then sell it back to them.
Principle 5: It is better to ask questions than make statements.	**Law 5:** Always ask at least six questions before making your first statement.
Principle 6: Communication has nothing to do with what is said, only with what is received.	**Law 6:** Always use the customer's words.
Principle 7: It's different strokes for different folks.	**Law 7:** Sell the way your customer buys.

Let's now have a closer look at the seven laws and the reasoning behind them:

Law 1: Always sell based on the customer's reasons, not your own

As I've said, people do things for their reasons, not yours and they always will.

It is really not important what you think.

The only thing that is important is what the customer thinks.

What you think is valuable may not be perceived in the same way by the customer.

What you think is important may be totally irrelevant to the buyer.

What you think is quality and what your customer thinks is quality may be worlds apart.

I am convinced that in this world you can get almost anything you want by first giving people what they want.

This law is hooked closely to Law 4, which we'll get to in a moment.

The only thing that's important is what the customer thinks is important.

Law 2: Your first job is to get people to like you

Selling is more about opening than closing.

The first thirty seconds are critical.

People instinctively decide in the first thirty seconds whether they are going to like you, or not. Whether they will feel comfortable with you, or not. Whether they will be able to trust you, or not.

The ability to create rapport (from the ancient Greek meaning: *to breathe together*) in the first thirty seconds is vital.

This one follows the old saying, 'show me you care before you tell me what you're selling.'

The feelings of the first thirty seconds will dictate the outcome of the last thirty seconds.

The feelings of the first thirty seconds will dictate the outcome of the last thirty seconds.

Law 3: Adapt quickly to your customer's style

People generally buy from people they trust and feel comfortable with.

People feel comfortable with people who are like them. Doves feel comfortable with Doves, Eagles feel comfortable with Eagles, Peacocks with Peacocks, Owls with Owls.

The ability to be able to adapt to other people's styles, in my opinion, dictates to a large degree how

People feel comfortable with people who are like them.

successful somebody will be in selling. Being able to adapt your style is the major thrust of this book.

Law 4: Find out what your customer is buying, then sell it back to them

This law is probably the most important thing I have ever learnt in selling.

When you use this one, you will rarely miss the sale.

Coupled with the principles of, 'People don't buy things, they buy how it will make them feel,' and 'People do things for their reasons, not yours,' it follows that when you can find out what your customer is buying, and then sell those aspects back to him, or her, you rarely miss a sale.

Law 5: Always ask at least six questions before making your first statement

I wish I knew about this one when I first went into selling. If I did, I would have made a lot more sales.

People buy from within – not from without.

In my opinion, external persuasion is a myth. People don't need to be sold they just need convincing. And the best people to convince them are themselves. And the best way to do this is with questions.

Questions get people to think – to go within. And when they go within - they sell themselves.

Statements made by another person (especially a salesperson) are generally taken with a pinch of salt.

Questions get people to think – to go within. And when they go within they sell themselves.

Unfortunately there are still many salespeople who believe that their job is to talk. To 'sell' the customer by pointing out the so-called features and benefits, overcome the objections and then 'do the close.'

It is as if the customer was somebody you had to do battle with. Whether this is right or wrong, one thing is for sure - it has never worked that way for me or for the people I have sold to.

Selling in the 1990s is more about counseling, consulting, being an expert, finding out who the customer is, what they want, and more importantly, why they want it, then advising and recommending. And the best way to do this is by asking questions.

Remember, we've just finished talking about *find out what your customer is buying, then sell it back to them*. Asking questions is an integral part of that process.

We'll go into asking questions a little deeper in chapter ten, but for now, remember: Always ask at least six questions before you make your first statement.

Law 6: Always use the customer's words

Communication has nothing to do with what is said, only with what is received. In other words, it only means what it means to the other person.

Words are only codes for mental pictures.

We all have our own mental picture for a word.

My picture for the word *safe* is probably different to your picture of the word *safe*. And if you are trying to sell me something, then your picture, and the meaning of the word *safe* is irrelevant. The only thing that matters is my picture and my meanings of the word.

Always use their dictionary and movie screen – not yours.

So, always use the exact words as those that your customer is using. If they use the word *cheap*, then you use the word *cheap*, not *economical*, not *bargain*, but *cheap*.

If they call it green and a blind man could see it's blue, then it's green. Always use their dictionary and movie screen — not yours.

Law 7: Sell the way your customer buys

It's different strokes for different folks. Hopefully, we've strongly established this fact by now; otherwise I've failed in the first part of this book!

It's different strokes for different folks.

How to go about selling the way your customer buys is coming soon. But before we get there, let's have a look first at being more like a doctor than a salesperson.

9

Be the Doctor

How to sell the way your customer buys is a consultative process.

It has more to do with acting like a doctor than it does with appearing like a salesperson.

Like a doctor, the approach looks more like a problem-solving exercise than it does a selling exercise.

And like a doctor's approach, the process basically involves five stages, and they are:

BE THE DOCTOR

1. **Ask questions**
2. **Listen well**
3. **Assess the problem**
4. **Diagnose the problem**
5. **Write the prescription**

1. Ask questions
They say that half the answer to any problem lies in knowing how to ask the right questions.

In my opinion, the ability to be able to ask the right questions and then be able to listen — and actually hear! — the answer, is most probably one of the most important skills a professional salesperson can have.

We have already talked about the principle of asking six questions before making your first statement. This is all part of the problem-solving-consultative process.

In the next chapter we'll have a close look at the art of using questions.

2. Listen well
Listening well requires patience. As a good friend of mine said not long ago, "God, give me patience and I

want it now!"

Another friend of mine says that, "Listening is an unnatural act performed by consenting adults."

Whatever listening is, it is fair to say that generally speaking, most of us salespeople are not particularly good at it — and it shows.

The following are twenty ways not to listen. Do a 'stocktake' on yourself and see how you score out of twenty for your ability *not* to listen:

Listening is an unnatural act performed by consenting adults.

1. Working out how to leave the conversation.
2. Checking your watch.
3. Looking at the scenery.
4. Preparing your next statement.
5. Thinking of what advice to give.
6. Bringing your own story into it.
7. Forming judgements about the speaker.
8. Finding flaws in the speaker's argument.
9. Arguing and debating.
10. Drifting off on your own agenda.
11. Interrupting with your opinion.
12. Providing too-quick answers and solutions.
13. Listening to only what applies to you.
14. Assuming what's going to be said.
15. Finishing the other person's sentences.
16. Wondering what's for dinner tonight.
17. Trying to be too nice — self-preoccupation.
18. Trying to change the subject.
19. Trying to control the conversation.
20. Trying to make the other person wrong.

What was that again?

Here are twelve tips for better listening:

1. Stop talking out loud.
2. Stop talking to yourself.
3. Centre yourself with the speaker.
4. Listen in silence and with full attention.
5. Don't prepare your next comment before the speaker has finished talking.

6. Listen for the feelings behind the words.
7. Tune in with your 'third ear' for what is not being said.
8. Avoid interrupting with your own opinion or story.
9. Watch the speaker's eyes, expressions and body language.
10. Put your personal judgements on hold.
11. Show you are actively listening.
12. Stop talking — I know it's the same as number one, but it's worth repeating!.

3. Assess the problem

A problem is the gap between where somebody is now and where they want to be.

A problem is the gap between where somebody is now and where they want to be.

If you have asked the right questions and listened well, by now you know the problem — that is, what your customer is really buying.

4. Diagnose the problem

As I've said, a problem is the gap between where somebody is and where they want to be.

Problem solving is about filling the gap.

Problem solving is about closing that gap.

Like a doctor, by now you are ready to fill the gap with a remedy by fitting your product or service to the problem — by providing an answer — a solution.

5. Write the prescription

Closing is the same as writing a prescription.

If you have followed the process carefully, if you have asked all the right questions, if you have assessed the problem well and diagnosed it correctly, then all that is left is to write the prescription — close the sale.

Remember, like a doctor, you are the expert in your field. Closing should be as automatic at this stage as a doctor writing a prescription.

We'll talk more about 'closing questions' in chapter eleven: Selling the Way Your Customer Buys.

For now, let's move to the Art of Using Questions.

FOOD FOR THOUGHT

If you continue
to do what
you have
always
done, you
will always
get what
you have
always got

10 The art of using questions

Mouth I've one and ears I've two
Well that's what I got the last count
Perhaps somebody is trying to tell me
I should use them in the same amount

Most salespeople talk too much.

Questions are the lifeblood of a professional salesperson.

Most salespeople talk too much.

Many salespeople would increase their sales by thirty per cent overnight if only they would learn to do three very basic things; learn to ask questions, then listen, then to look as if they're listening.

When you're talking you don't learn anything.

Law 1 says; 'Always sell based on the customer's reasons, not your own.'

Law 4 says; 'Find out what your customer is buying, then sell it back to them.'

The only way you will find these things out is by asking questions.

In the words of Rudyard Kipling;

I keep six serving honest men
They taught me all I knew
Their names are what
And when and how
And why and where and who.

When you're talking you don't learn anything.

If you want someone to think about something and become actively involved in a conversation, then give them a question, not an answer.

Some of the best questions you can ask

Remember to start your questions with Rudyard Kipling's 'honest men.' What, when, how, why, where and who.

As a general rule, these will make your questions open. Open questions prompt dialogue. Dialogue gets you information.

Again, as a general rule, questions not starting with the 'honest men' will be closed questions and all they will get you is a brief 'yes' or 'no' or even a shrug, or a grunt. You don't learn much from a shrug or a grunt.

Avoid the 'Why?' question – it gets peoples' backs up.

A word of warning: it pays to avoid the 'why' question. 'Why' is confrontational and challenging. 'Why' is what mothers and fathers and teachers ask!

Later I'll give you a 'softer' substitute for the 'why-question.' Now, here are six of the best:

1. What do you want it to do for you?
This is a great question for finding out quickly just what the customer is buying (so you can sell it back to him, or her).

2. What else do you want it to do for you?
I find you don't really get to the nitty gritty of the true underlying reasons until you have asked this one.

3. Can you tell me more?
I know it's a closed question, but it works as a nice 'piggy back' question to 'what else do you want it to for you?' if the answer has been too brief.

4. I'm not sure I get your meaning. Can you say that in another way.

Again, another 'piggy back' question for getting the true underlying reasons for buying, or use its first cousin:

5. I'm sorry, can you run that past me again? I don't think I'm with you.

Or a variation of the same theme.

6. What makes you say that?

This is the 'all purpose tool' for any salesperson worth their salt.

It can be used in almost any situation and at almost any time.

It's the 'soft' substitute for the why-question which can often get people's backs up.

"What makes you say that?" keeps you neutral.

It's a marvelous tool, especially when dealing with what might sound like an objection.

If you answer an objection with a statement you have immediately taken sides. 'What makes you say that' keeps you neutral — which is where you want to be — unless you want to win the war and lose the battle.

The Golden rule is: 'Never defend until you have found out what is really behind the objection'.

"It's a bit expensive isn't it!"

"What makes you say that?"

Never defend until you have found out what is really behind the objection.

The answer you get will get you very valuable information in the form of opinions, values, and more importantly the customer's budget constraints.

"I don't think this is right for us."

"What makes you say that?"

The answer you get on this one will give you exactly what the customer wants to buy so that if you can, you can sell it back to them.

"Nah, we've tried that before and it didn't work."

"What makes you say that?"

I'm sure you're getting the picture.

You may have gathered by now that I like 'What makes you say that?'

Here are just some of the reasons why I like it and why it works — which is the main thing.

♦ It keeps you neutral.
♦ It's non-confronting.
♦ It cannot be answered with one word.
♦ It forces people to think.
♦ It forces people to talk.
♦ It forces you to listen.
♦ It brings things out into the open.
♦ It gets you the information you need to know to be able to sell effectively.

To wrap up

Find out what your customer is buying and sell it back to them. You can only do that by asking good questions.

Oh, and by the way, after each question, wait at least six seconds before you open your mouth again. Suppress the urge to talk and fill the silence.

Wait at least six seconds before engaging the mouth again.

When you can ask six questions before making your first statement, when you can wait for at least six seconds before saying anything else, when you can do that, you can pass go and collect $200 — you have learnt the art of asking questions.

Armed with the ability to ask the right questions and listen well, let's move now to Selling the Way Your Customer Buys.

FOOD FOR THOUGHT

People do
things for
their reasons
not yours

And they
always will

Selling the way your customer buys

11

It has been said that people don't really buy — they choose.

How to Sell the Way Your Customer Buys is about helping people to choose your product or service.

As I've said before, it is a consultative process. How to Sell the Way Your Customer Buys has more to do with solving problems than it does with manipulation or persuasion.

To suggest that there is only one way to sell is to suggest that everybody is the same, and that is ridiculous.

People are different and therefore need to be treated differently.

How to Sell the Way Your Customer Buys is about recognising that difference and being able to respond to it.

It's about breaking down barriers. It's about adapting to your customer's style, being able to move into their world, being able to better understand them and their needs better, and being able to relate to, and communicate with them more effectively in order to produce a win-win outcome.

It should also be noted that the tips, approaches and strategies given here apply just as equally for a written presentation as they do for a verbal presentation.

People don't really buy, they choose

People are different.

How to Sell the Way Your Customer Buys is about recognising the difference and being able to respond to it

Meet the Peacock again

Appears	Confident, outgoing, friendly and warm. A talker.
Speed	Fast and impulsive.
Dress	Stylish, colourful, designer labels, flamboyant.
Face	Open, expressive and cheerful.
Acts	Relaxed and friendly.
Communicates	Outspoken, unselfconscious, fast and expressive.
Motivated By	Recognition, applause, status symbols, fame.
Work Space	Plaques, certificates, photos, 'image' artifacts.
Theme Song	"Hey world – look at me!"
Under Pressure	Becomes noisy and dramatic — then wants to be friends.

Selling to the Peacock

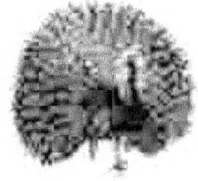

Worries About	How they look to others — their image. This includes their appearance, their job, their house, their car — everything about them.
Buys	They buy what makes them happy. Especially anything that makes them look good — prestige, reputation, showiness. They will go into debt to look good.
Their Approach to Buying	They love buying. They are impulsive and intuitive. If it feels good, do it. Often price is not a problem — until after they've had a chance to think about it. They are ready — fire — aim — buyers.
Be Prepared	Be prepared to do lots of listening and nodding. Be prepared to keep him, or her, on track by asking questions. Be prepared with something to look at and demonstrate as they are very visual people. Be prepared to let them touch and feel and 'play with' the product. Involve them in any way you can.
Your Approach	Fast, warm and friendly — and with enthusiasm. Be careful of your own appearance — dress well.
Open With	Talk that focuses on them — and their accomplishments. "What have you been up to lately?" "How long have you been the sales manager here?" "Do you find this job challenging?" "What do you think of it?" (If they were already looking before you approached them).

Creating Comfort	Get them to talk about opinions and ideas — it won't be hard!
Building Common Ground	Be optimistic, don't take life too seriously — they don't. Share your ideas. Be imaginative. Be entertaining. Get excited.
Focus On	How it will add to their prestige, reputation etc. How other people will see and feel about what it is they are buying.
Creating Interest	Tell them about the important people and companies who have dealt with you, or have bought your product. Use testimonials — name drop a little.
Presentation Strategies	Talk concepts and broad principles first before going deeper. Use lots of 'show and tell' demonstration. You'll have more luck dealing with them face to face than you will sending them something to look at, or read. They are not big readers and get bored with details. If you must send them something on paper, make sure they have no more than one page to read. Then follow-up quickly.
Hot-Button Words and Phrases	New, the latest, faster, quicker, stylish, exciting, state of the art, leading edge, easy, unique, simple to use.
Don'ts	Don't get too analytical — if at all. Don't criticise their opinions or choices. Don't go into any fine detail unless they want to. Don't try and debate with them. You might win the battle, but you will lose the war.
Closing Comments	"Shall we get the show on the road?" "What do you reckon — is it a goer?" "What do you think — shall we do it?"
Your Challenge	Your challenge will be keeping them focused on the job at hand. They will go off on tangents. Keep them on track by bringing them back to the point with questions — as they take a breath!

Beware	Make sure you are both abundantly clear and in full agreement concerning the action that needs to be taken on the details of the what, when, who, how and where. Put it on paper. Confirm everything in writing. They have a marvelous capacity for saying things like, "I can't remember saying, or agreeing, to that."
In A Nutshell	The Peacock is usually an 'easy buyer' if handled correctly. They will talk the leg off a chair. Bight your tongue and do a lot of listening. Get excited. Appeal to their ego and relate what you are selling to its 'image value'. Use a 'show and tell' selling approach. Make sure you are both clear on the details before closing. Try and keep the transaction as 'paper free' as possible.
And Another Thing	Offer to do all the paperwork for them. They hate anything that looks like paperwork, or smells of 'administration work.' Praise their buying decision after the sale.

Meet the Dove again

Appears	Shy, friendly, warm, quiet. A feeler.
Speed	Slow — unobtrusive — low key.
Dress	Pastel to bright colours, but not outlandish.
Face	Open but bashful. Expressions reflect what you are saying.
Acts	Like a friendly listener.
Communicates	Calmly, softly-spoken, self-conscious. Easy to talk to.
Motivated By	Acceptance, approval, belonging. Peace and harmony.
Work Space	Friendly, homely, sociable. Plants and family photograph.
Theme Song	"We all need each other — let's save the whales."
Under Pressure	Withdraws, goes quiet, then gets stubborn.

Selling to the Dove

Worries About	What other people will think of them.
	That they will buy the wrong thing.
	That they will be embarrassed.
Buys	They buy what makes other people happy.
	They also buy what everybody else is buying.
	They want to fit in, to not stand out in the crowd.
	They are not risk-takers or adventurers.
Their Approach to Buying	Because they are not naturally quick decision makers they are not quick or impulsive buyers.
	They need help and personal reassurances of support that they are 'doing the right thing.'
Be Prepared	Be prepared to take it slow and easy.
	Be prepared to explore the feelings behind the purchase.
	Be prepared to listen — and show you are listening.
	Be prepared to back-up your claims with how other buyers have been happy with the product.
Your Approach	Casual, warm, calm and friendly.
	Bring them out with questions to explore the feelings behind the purchase.
Open With	Talk that focuses on helping and feelings.
	"How can I help?"
	"How do you feel about that one?"
	"Is this the sort of thing you have been looking for?"
	"This is very popular, most people choose it."

Creating Comfort	Show you are open to conversation. Be interested in them as a person.
Building Common Ground	Talk family and friendships — 'people talk.'
Focus On	How other people will feel about what it is they are buying.
Creating Interest	Tell them about how the other people and companies who have dealt with you, or have bought your product, feel about it and are happy with it.
Presentation Strategies	Support their feelings and opinions. Give them plenty of time to spell out what they want and why they want it. Explore areas of dissatisfaction — they won't tell you unless you ask. Get agreement at each step before progressing any further. Lay out the steps they need to take to make the decision easier.
Hot-Button Words and Phrases	Trust, safe, genuine, comfortable, approved, service, satisfaction, bargain, value, looks right, this is the one for you.
Don'ts	Don't try and push a new idea. Don't criticise their opinions or choices. Don't go into any fine detail unless they want to. Don't try and close them too soon — don't push them.
Closing Comments	"This seems to be the right one for you — shall we go ahead with this one then?" "Are you happy to go ahead with this one?" "Let's go ahead then — shall we?"
Your Challenge	Your challenge will be in having patience. Slowing down. Not rushing them. Being prepared to talk about what you may think are irrelevant issues. Not appearing like a 'pushy salesperson,' which they are very wary of and will try and avoid.

Beware	Don't rush them. Don't come on too strong. Offer assurances and 'safety nets,' but don't overstate your guarantees, or you will lose their trust — which is what they intuitively operate on. They can smell a phoney at a hundred paces.
In A Nutshell	The Dove is a very friendly and easygoing person. They are easy to relate to and talk to. But don't let this easygoing nature put you into a false sense of security. If they feel they are being 'snowed' or pushed into something they don't feel right about, they will thank you nicely for your trouble and quietly, but quickly, exit the scene. The second-to-last thing they want is to be pushed into something that doesn't feel right to them. The very last thing they want is to be embarrased by being in that situation.
And Another Thing	Do the 'right thing' by the Dove and you will have a customer and an advocate for life. They will always return to places and people who they can trust and where they feel comfortable and well treated. And they will never return to where they are not — and you will never know why because they will never tell you. That would be embarrassing.

Meet the Eagle again

Appears	Confident, assertive, cool and distant. A doer.
Speed	Fast — no nonsense.
Dress	Darker colours, smart but conservative.
Face	Set and determined, gives little away.
Acts	In a quick and businesslike manner.
Communicates	Strong voice, quick, abrupt, to the point.
Motivated By	Challenge, action, competition, getting results.
Work Space	Unadorned, no frills, businesslike.
Theme Song	"Winning isn't everything — it's the only thing."
Under Pressure	Bossy and sarcastic, then avoids the situation or person.

Selling to the Eagle

Worries About	Not having control. Not getting the results they want.
Buys	Anything which gives them results, status, or commands respect. (Think of an armour-plated Range Rover!)
Their Approach to Buying	As with everything else they do, their approach is quick and decisive. Like the bird itself, they know what they want and swoop on it. They are certainly not 'look, touch and feel' shoppers. They buy as if they were attacking a village!
Be Prepared	Be prepared to do the business quickly. Be prepared to take a subordinate position when selling to them — but don't come over as 'wimpy.' Be prepared to show that you know that their time is important to them. Be prepared to know the facts and to be able to deliver them quickly and concisely.
Your Approach	Fast, concise and businesslike. Give them your full attention — don't get distracted with other things. Focus on what they are focusing on — don't offer alternatives without being asked to offer them.
Open With	Talk that focuses on getting results. Get to the point fast. "How can I help you?" "What are you looking for?" "What do you want it to do for you?"

Creating Comfort	Avoid familiarity. Avoid trying to be witty. Get to the point quickly.
Building Common Ground	Talk outcomes and results — theirs.
Focus On	What they want it to do for them.
Creating Interest	Tell them about how the other people and companies who have dealt with you, or have bought your product have got the results they were looking for.
Presentation Strategies	Don't beat around the bush. Ask — don't tell. Establish their goals quickly and then talk around those goals. Stick to business — no small talk. Argue the facts — not your personal opinions. Be assertive and forthright.
Hot-Button Words and Phrases	Results, performance, control, bottom line, quick, fast, simple, reliable, effective, productive, profitable.
Don'ts	Don't waste their time. Don't go into detail unless they ask for it. Don't try and up-sell them. Don't try and close them unless you are absolutely sure they are ready to go ahead.
Closing Comments	"What is your decision?" "Have you made your decision?" "What have you decided on?" "Are you ready to go ahead now?"
Your Challenge	Your challenge will be in taking a subordinate role. Asking precise questions, rather than making 'selling statements.' Eagles want status, respect, authority and results — they want to be the boss — especially in a 'selling situation.' Let them appear to have full control. Do the business quickly and efficiently.

Beware	You will lose them, and the sale, if you take too long over it, or try to dazzle them with science or details, or in any way try to bluff them.
In A Nutshell	The Eagle is fast, aggressive and abrupt. They are quick and decisive. They know what they want with no 'messing about.' They are good people to do business with as long as you keep it on a strictly businesslike basis.
And Another Thing	They put little stock in business relationships. It is almost pointless trying to build up a relationship with an Eagle in the hope that the relationship will count for their 'customer loyalty.' Eagles don't operate that way. The relationship will only last for as long as the Eagle is getting what it wants. If you come between what the Eagle wants and what the Eagle has got, you will be the casualty of the relationship you thought you had — but never did. Sentiment is not one of their long suits.

Meet the Owl again

Appears	Quiet, conservative, reserved. A thinker.
Speed	Slow and deliberate.
Dress	Browns and autumn colours, very conservative.
Face	Expressionless — poker face — sometimes grim.
Acts	Quiet and withdrawn, preoccupied with something else.
Communicates	Softly spoken, unemotional, detached, preoccupied.
Motivated By	Procedures, information, rules, predictability.
Work Space	Orderly, sterile, organised, impersonal.
Theme Song	"Fools rush in where wise men fear to tread."
Under Pressure	Becomes quietly critical and then withdraws within.

Selling to the Owl

Worries About	Not being right. Making the wrong decision.
Buys	They buy what is safe — the tried and proven.
Their Approach to Buying	They are far from being quick, or impulsive buyers. They are traditionalists — they are not open to new ideas. They have normally done lots of extensive homework, in fact they might know more about your product than you do! Don't be surprised if they quote 'Choice' magazine, or the latest technical up-date.
Be Prepared	Be prepared to take it slow and easy. Be prepared to be systematic, organised and thoroughly prepared with all the facts. Be prepared to have brochures and technical catalogues to give to them. Be prepared to list the pros and cons of any plan you suggest and have viable alternatives for dealing with the disadvantages.
Your Approach	Slow, precise, logical and businesslike. Avoid attempts at humour. Avoid small talk of a personal nature.
Open With	Talk that focuses on reassurance. "This particular one has a total after-sales back-up service." "This model is fully guaranteed." "We never have call-backs with this one — it is totally reliable."

Creating Comfort	Avoid familiarity. Avoid humour — they see it as frivolous.
Building Common Ground	Be impersonal. Talk about tasks — not people. Stick to the job at hand.
Focus On	Reliability. No risk.
Creating Interest	Tell them about how the other people and companies who have dealt with you, or have bought your product, have been happy with the reliability and after-sales service. Offer to provide testimonials as proof.
Presentation Strategies	Keep it impersonal — stick to business. Provide solid factual evidence, not personal opinion, to back up what you say. Give them plenty of time to think before expecting a response. Offer reassurances of guarantees and warranties where possible.
Hot-Button Words and Phrases	Tried and proven, reliable, will never let you down, guaranteed, comes with a full warranty, tested, economical.
Don'ts	Don't rush them — in fact, don't even think about it! Don't fill their thinking-time with silence (which can be quite long) with your talking.
Closing Comments	"This seems to be the right one — shall we go ahead with it?" "Are you ready to go ahead with this one?" "This one seems to have everything you're looking for — do you want to go ahead?"
Your Challenge	Your challenge will be in taking a slow, logical, and systematic approach. Not talking while they're thinking because you find the silence 'deafening.' Being amiable and patient while going into the depth and the amount of details they want to go into. Wanting to close too early. Getting frustrated when you feel it has all been talked out and then they say (which they sincerely mean) "Let me sleep on it for a while."

Beware	Don't try and rush them for a decision, otherwise you will get a 'no' that could well have been a 'yes' if you had given them more time to think about it.
In A Nutshell	Owls are cautious pessimists. They totally believe in Murphy's Law, 'If anything can go wrong, it will.' They are always second guessing themselves — and everybody else. You need to take it slow and steady with lots of facts and details to back up your claims — and make sure they're on paper. If it's not on paper then it can't be right as far as the Owl is concerned.
And Another Thing	Owls are very frugal people, which means they give a dollar a very good home! But they can surprise you. On the one hand they will pay as least as possible for something, yet on the other they will pay a small fortune for the 'best brand' stereo equipment, or the like. Perhaps it's because they love perfection.
	Oh, and one more thing; send your proposals to them before any meeting so that they can have the time to analyse it quietly and privately. This way you have a far better chance of your meeting with them having a productive outcome.

12 A final word before we close

We communicate with the world the way we want to be communicated to.

This is the 'Big Message'.

Before you can walk in another's shoes, you have to take your own off first.

Intelligence, they say, is the ability to quickly adapt to one's environment. It follows then, that intelligent salespeople are quick adapters.

They adapt quickly to their customer's style, and by adapting to their customer's style, they create trust and comfort.

We are comfortable with people who are like us. Most of the friends we choose are of a similar style to our own for this reason.

People will tell you who they are by the way they communicate with the world.

We communicate to the world the way we want to be communicated to.

Intelligent salespeople know this and adapt their style to suit.

This is the basic 'Big Message' of this little book:

When you are with a Peacock, become a Peacock.

When you are with a Dove, become a Dove.

When you are with an Eagle, become an Eagle.

When you are with an Owl, become an Owl.

When you do this, you will move into their world.

You will be displaying 'empathy in action'. 'Empathy', by the way, is the ability to walk in another's shoes — but you have to take your own off first.

When you can move into another's world, when you can see the world as they see it, when you can feel what they are feeling, when you can appreciate what they value, and what they don't, you will have mastered the art of How to Sell the Way Your Customer Buys.

The Winner's Edge

The gap between the winners and the also-rans is not a big one.

In fact it's a very narrow one.

In sport, for instance, it's measured in milimeters and fractions of a second.

In professional golf, one stroke can be the difference between winning a million dollars or getting appearance money.

So, what makes a winner a winner in any field of endeavour?

The answer, simply put, is that winners do the things the also-rans don't do, can't do, or don't want to do.

Winners do the things the others don't do.

One of the things that winning salespeople do that the also-rans don't do, is that they adapt quickly to the person they're selling to — but we've talked enough about that. You get the point.

Results are all that count

My experience tells me that people who are average often work harder than those who excell.

One of the reasons I find for this is that those who work hard, but seem to get nowhere, tend to measure themselves by the amount of activity, or 'busy-ness' that they're involved in.

On the other hand, my experience also shows me that those who excell have only one measure — and that's the results they achieve. Results are all that count to them.

Nobody cares how often we try.

When you think about it, nobody really cares how often we try. They're only interested in how often we succeed — they're only interested in results.

Coming close only counts in dancing.

So, keep on doing what the others don't do, can't do, or don't want to do.

Be a winner — get results.

Cheers.

Other Titles by Des Hunt

What Makes People Tick?
By Des Hunt
ISBN: 9780992555344
Genre: Non-fiction/self-help/personality
Publisher: AWC Business Solutions
www.tick.com.au

Available in print and ebook

This is Australia's quiet best-selling book and practical guide to self-discovery and personal growth. In it you will discover:

* Your own personality style and the style of those you live and work with
* How to see yourself as others see you
* The strengths, shortcomings and hidden talents of the different styles
* What style is best suited to what job
* How to pick another's style within 30 seconds of meeting them.
* How to relate better with others
* How to avoid personality clashes
* How to enrich your relationships

What Makes People Tick contains a unique, quick and easy-to-complete questionnaire to discover personality types as well as a Job Compatibility Indicator to pinpoint the most suitable personality type for each occupation. *What Makes People Tick* is 'must know' information for people who have to deal with, live with, sell to, and generally get on with other people.